CREATIVE RESPONSIBILITY

BY

C. Thomas Sikking

DeVorss & Company, Publishers
P.O. Box 550
Marina del Rey, California 90291

Second Printing 1981

ISBN: 0-87516-389-0

U.S. Library of Congress Catalog Number: 79-55974

Printed in the United States of America by
Book Graphics, Inc., Marina del Rey, California

For Betty

Contents

INTRODUCTION   vii

    I THE BUCK STOPS HERE   1

   II THE BUILDING BLOCKS   8

  III THE CREATIVE YOU   13

  IV THE CREATED YOU   18

    V USING CREATIVE TOOLS   23

  VI GOALS   30

 VII CREATIVE HABITS   39

VIII CREATING THROUGH CONFLICT   45

  IX CREATING OUT OF HURT   53

    X A PRICELESS GIFT   57

  XI CREATING HEALTH   66

 XII PROSPERITY   72

XIII CREATING PROSPERITY   77

XIV HAPPINESS NEVER "HAPPENS"   83

 XV RELAX—BE COOL   89

Introduction

O NE OF MY psychiatric professors once said that if you sit the leading proponents of all the major systems of psychotherapy down at one table and watch each of them work with people, they all treat their patients the same way, but use different words to describe their own system of therapy.

In this same way the author has extracted the common denominator from all the "success and how-to books," and in a very simple and straight-forward way he has projected an easily learned way of controlling our life experience, instead of allowing the experience of life to control us.

Creative Responsibility does not delve into religion. It simply assumes a creative force in the universe, and it beautifully describes the meeting-ground between our inner and outer reality. Reading this book will give you a sense of freedom as well as responsibility for your life. I feel this is one of the important lessons we can learn from life.

As I read this book I kept thinking of Matt. 6:21: "Where your treasure is, there will your heart be also." What you think is valuable or important is where your mind dwells.

John D. Bischel, M.D.

I

The Buck Stops Here

MILLIONS OF WORDS have been written and spoken about how to have a better life, more money in the bank, a healthier body, more harmonious personal relationships, or whatever a "better life" may mean to an individual. Most of these books and lectures contain valid and workable techniques for attaining the "better life." Yet, how many people are seeing evidence of significant changes in their lives even after being exposed to those techniques? Not nearly enough!

There is a thread of consistency that runs through those millions of words that seems either to be missed altogether or is given a secondary place to the value of the book or the lecture. The thread or theme is what we will call "creative responsibility."

CREATIVE RESPONSIBILITY

Creative responsibility is the key to a better life experience! Creative responsibility is not something we need to attain. We already have it, but we should learn to use it more often and more effectively. We all have the ability to respond, and we do it all day long. Life is a series of responses. We respond to the alarm clock first thing in the morning. Then we respond to a hunger pang and go eat breakfast. The rest of the day is spent in responding to other people, to sounds, the written word, odors, and all of the activities that go into making up our world. We also respond to our own thoughts and feelings. The vital thing we must learn to do more often and more effectively is to make sure those responses are *creative*. We want to make certain that our responses *create* what we want in life; not what we don't want! When we attain and keep an attitude of *creative responsibility,* our lives can only change for the better.

The late Harry S. Truman, when he was president of the United States, had a sign on his desk that received considerable comment from the press. It read simply, ''The buck stops here.'' Mr. Truman didn't coin the phrase; it had been around for years. Military servicemen have talked of "passing the buck" and discussed "where the buck stops" down through the years. We know that the word buck, in this case, means blame, and we are all "buck passers" to greater or lesser degrees. It seems to be far easier and less damaging to our ego to find a scapegoat for our failures, big and small. We pass the buck to our parents, local prejudices, the economy, our employer, the government or world affairs in general. Yet, we are only fooling ourselves and prolonging the situations in which we find ourselves.

It is time to stop passing the buck! If we continue to place the blame on something or someone else, we avoid making any changes within ourselves. And if our lives, worlds, and personal circumstances are to be changed for the better, then *we* must accept the responsibility.

The hard fact is that you are where you are socially, financially, emotionally, and physically because of your own thinking processes up to this point. What you will be in the future will be determined by your own mental activity now. If your thinking process does not change significantly, neither will your life and life-style. Change your thinking patterns and you change what you are. Most psychiatrists and psychologists agree that people tend to become exactly as they imagine themselves to be. It follows then, that if you change your thinking habits, you change what you are.

Some three thousand years ago, a wise man by the name of Solomon said, "For as he thinketh in his heart, so is he. . . ." The concept of a man being the product of his own thinking is certainly not a new or unique one. Of the tens of thousands of words written on the subject, many books continue year after year to be popular sellers. PSCHO-CYBERNETICS by Dr. Maxwell Maltz, and THE POWER OF POSITIVE THINKING by Dr. Norman Vincent Peale, are but two of many that fall into this category. We read these books and say, "That is a great book! It's a very practical concept that could change the world." Then we put the book back on the shelf, along with many others we have read and do little or nothing about changing our thinking.

Around the turn of the nineteenth century, a German poet and philosopher said, "All truly wise thoughts have been thought already thousands of times; but to make them truly ours, we must think them over again honestly, till they take root in our personal experience." Surely the time has come to do something about our lives; change them into what we desire them to be. Waiting for the government, religion, the economy, the leaders of the world or just the other guy to change things for us is a waste of time. Not only is it a waste of time, but up to this point it hasn't worked very well. It is time to stop passing the buck. Each and every one of us must place a sign on the "desk" of his mind, that simply says, "The buck stops here." The time has come for us to accept the responsibility for ourselves and our world, because in truth, this is where the ultimate responsibility lies.

As human beings, we are unique among all of God's creations. We can *choose* what we will think or think about. Individually, we have dominion over our thoughts and can change their direction at will. The fact that we can change the direction of our thought is most important.

As children our dominion is quite limited, and we accept from our parents, teachers, and elders, all kinds of information and facts that may or may not be true. If a woman goes through a bitter divorce, she might very easily pass on, in word and deed, to her young daughter a deep distrust of men. Now if somewhere along the line this daughter does not change this idea of men, she could find herself a very unhappy adult. So in a sense, we can see that a child may have a valid excuse to pass the buck. As an adult, with a mature reasoning faculty, there is no excuse. There is no excuse because the adult has the ability to change the direction of his thinking *if* he so chooses.

One of the greatest areas in which we tend to "pass the buck" is where other people, events, or circumstances seem to keep us from doing what we want to do, or being what we want to be. These are the times when we blame the government, our spouse, our employer, or the economy for our failures or shortcomings. Yet, this is not valid.

Things, people, circumstances, and events do *not* affect you. What does affect you is your reaction to or opinion of those things, people, circumstances, or events. And you either choose your reaction or you react out of a previously formed habit of thinking. But remember, *you* can *change* your thinking: you can form new thinking habits.

So often it is said, "She hurt my feelings," or "I'm sorry I hurt your feelings." Yet, you cannot hurt someone else's feelings, nor can they hurt yours. They hurt their own feelings. They choose to react to your words and actions, and your feelings are hurt in exactly the same way, by your chosen reaction.

We read some statistics that say a high school graduate will average only so many dollars a year in income. We accept the concept; it becomes our frame of reference, and then we blame our lack of higher education for our mediocrity. That is passing the buck.

What people think about most of the time is what they are. People say, "That can't be true. I think about money all the time, but I never have enough." Yet, under closer examination, we find that it is not *just* money they think about all the time; it is the *lack* of money. We will be discussing this subject of money in detail in a following chapter. We make these same choices when it comes to our health. Generally speaking, we are about as healthy or unhealthy as we expect to be.

The excuses and rationalizations are too numerous to count, and we all use them—but they are not valid. They may have some validity for our past, but they have nothing to do with our circumstance from this day forward. There is no longer any excuse to "pass the buck." The medical doctors, the psychiatrists, and psychologists are agreeing more and more. They have proved and continue to prove what great thinkers and teachers have been saying down through the ages: Man is the product of his own thinking! Only through changes in thinking can the end product be changed.

All too often "man" agrees with this concept, but "man" wants to wait until "man" changes. It is time to stop thinking in terms of "man" and think in terms of *you*. Yes, YOU, the one reading these words at this moment. Stop passing the buck! It stops here with you! If we all wait for "man" to change, we may wait for a long, long time. Why wait? You can change your life, beginning now. Accept the responsibility for your life and circumstance, because the buck stops here. Your life, circumstance, and future are solely *your* responsibility.

In the chapters that follow, many facets of life and circumstance will be discussed and practical ways of change outlined. But reading the words won't change things much. Remember — "the buck stops here," and it is up to you. Use your CREATIVE RESPONSE-ABILITY!

II

The Building Blocks

THE BUILDING BLOCKS of your life, your world, and
our world can be summed up in one word . . .
consciousness. In this text, the word "consciousness" is defined in its broadest sense. It is *not*
limited to a spiritual, religious, or esoteric definition.
"Consciousness" is simply the sum total of mental
activity and reserve. Your personal consciousness is
made up of everything you have ever thought or
experienced and most importantly everything you are
currently thinking and thinking about. Each personal
consciousness is unique simply because no two people
can experience totally identical experiences throughout their lives.

You always have your own individual consciousness that is unique, yet you are a part of a number of
"group consciousnesses." Any functioning group of
people automatically forms a "group consciousness"
such as a family consciousness. This is simply the
collective mind-action of the family. The character of
the family consciousness is established by the predominant thought patterns and habits of that family.

In much the same way a neighborhood, city, state, or national consciousness is established.

A group consciousness is sometimes quite easy to detect. You can walk into one family group and be aware of a good "feel." On the surface, the family may appear to be very much like most other families, and yet you sense something positive, vital, and balanced within the group. The predominant thought patterns and habits of that family are positive, vital, and balanced. By the same token, what you detect in a neighboring family may "feel" just the opposite. Once again, the predominant thought patterns and thought habits show their character.

You have probably gone into a city or town for the first time and then left saying, "That is such a nice town. Everyone was so friendly and it seemed so peaceful." Here again is a group consciousness in expression. Every city has its consciousness, and whether it is judged good, bad, or indifferent, it is reflecting the predominant thoughts of the folks living there.

There is another group consciousness of which we are all a part, and that is called the "race consciousness." Our world is in its present state as a result of the collective mental activity of all the people in our world. And what we see in our world is the outpicturing of the predominant thought patterns of the people of the world.

Do you like everything you see in our world? Of course not! You would like to see a better world just as everyone else would. Unfortunately you can't make the race consciousness change all at once.

To change any group consciousness, the changes must begin with the foundation, the individual consciousness. Each time one individual changes his consciousness, the group consciousness changes too. Perhaps not much change is evident in a larger group consciousness, but the change *is* there. As the song that has become popular in recent years says: "Let there be peace on earth and let it begin with me." If there is to be a change in "family consciousness," "city consciousness," or the "race consciousness," the change must begin with the individual's consciousness. *You!* The buck stops here!

Don't try to change your family, your town, or your world . . . change YOU!

The only way you can change YOU is to consciously change how you think and what you think about. You are the product of what you think. Change what you think and you change the product.

The best way to analyze your own thought patterns and thinking habits is to look at your life up to this point. Ask yourself some questions:

Am I as happy as I would like to be?

Am I completely satisfied with my income?

Am I as healthy as I want to be?

Am I content with my 'lot' in life?

Is there enough peace and love in my life?

Am I successful?

Do I deserve to have a better life?

Do I have the kind of life I *really* want?

If in the secret recesses of your mind, you answered all of these questions honestly and all the answers were "yes," then close this book and put it down. You don't need it. If any of the answers were "no," then read on. You have some work to do. It is time to put your creative responsibility into action. It is time to evaluate what you are thinking and make some changes.

The permanent things of this world in which you live are *not* in the physical realm. The permanent world is in the realm of *mind*. It is only in the realm of mind that anything has permanence and only from the realm of mind can anything be produced.

Everything you see about you was first an idea in the mind of man or in the mind of man's Creator.

Only in the realm of mind does anything have true permanence. The chair on which you sit, the house in which you live, and the Rock of Gibraltar can all be destroyed physically but remain untouched as ideas in the realm of mind.

It is through the activity of your mind that you bring about changes in your physical world. The mind-activity that must be dealt with is in the area of responses. If you want changes in your life experience, you have to change your habits of response to both outer and inner stimuli.

Outer stimuli are all of those things in your world that you experience (and to which you usually respond) through any of your physical senses: sight, touch, smell, hearing, and taste. Inner stimuli are those ideas and thoughts from within you.

Most of the time you respond from old thought habits with very little conscious thought. Many of these responses are valid and have a constructive place in your life; for example, if your hand touches a hot stove, you respond without conscious thought. If you are a long-time non-smoker and someone offers you a cigarette, your response is almost automatic, "No thank you." These are valid and creative responses that help you to have what *you* want in your life. If throughout your life, you have had less than a prosperous style of living, you may very likely have an "I can't afford" response that is a habit of long standing. As a result, your responses relative to money will be an automatic "I can't afford" and this is a destructive response. It will continue to help you have what you *don't* want in your life.

Remember—you are what you think about. In the above instance, "unable to afford."

You decide what you will think and how you will respond to any stimulus. You are in charge and no one can think or respond for you. Decide creatively and your life can change dramatically. It is up to you—the buck stops here! The consciousness you are building today will shape and mold your tomorrow.

II

The Creative You

THERE IS A creative process going on in you all the time. It doesn't stop even when you sleep. The process takes place, for the most part, in two phases or compartments of your mind: the conscious mind and the subconscious mind.

CONSCIOUS MIND

Your conscious mind is like the executive offices of a large manufacturing firm. This is where all of the decisions are made, goals are chosen, and value judgments are established. This is the part of you that receives information from all five of your physical senses; labels that information as good or bad, pleasant or unpleasant, true or false, sad or happy; and passes it on to the subconscious. Your conscious mind can also receive information from the subconscious mind, analyze it, ignore it, reconsider it, judge it, act on it, or send it back to the subconscious.

In the realm of the conscious mind *you* are in charge. You are the top executive. You can set the goals and make whatever value judgments you choose. The activity in the executive office (conscious mind) determines what kind of product (life) is going to be produced by the manufacturing department (subconscious) of the firm. Your conscious mind is the key to bringing about change in your life. You must learn to use it and use it creatively.

SUBCONSCIOUS MIND

The basic function of the subconscious mind is two-fold. First, it is your memory bank which stores up an image or remembrance of *everything* you experience through any one of your senses. All of the experiences are stored away, along with your feelings about each experience. Apparently, and from studies made of the subconscious, you remember everything. At any given time you may not recall everything that is stored there, but it is all in there! Everything can be recalled as well as the feelings that were experienced.

Dr. Wilder Penfield, who is a well-known neurosurgeon, discovered some very exciting things about the memory. Using an electric probe to stimulate a brain cell, his subjects clearly recalled long forgotten, specific experiences, complete with the emotion that went along with each particular event.

Your subconscious mind is a vast storehouse of specific information, much of which you do not recall consciously. For the sake of this discussion, part of your subconscious mind is a large warehouse for *your* manufacturing firm.

The second function of your subconscious mind is the actual manufacturing process that produces your life. And it works under the direction of your conscious mind. It is a creative activity constantly working to achieve goals. It is totally success oriented. The most important thing to keep in mind about your subconscious is that it makes *NO* value judgments. Its sole function is to achieve goals fed to it by the conscious mind.

Give your subconscious mind a positive or "successful" goal and it will achieve it. Because it makes no judgments, it will succeed in achieving a negative or "failure" goal just as quickly. If you do not give it a goal, it will seek out a goal it has achieved in the past and undertake to achieve it again. Remember, your subconscious is always at work, endeavoring to attain goals, and it is highly successful. Make certain that it is working to attain what you *want* in life, not what you *do not want*. Anytime that you feed data that is negative, such as:

> "I am unworthy."
> "I can't afford...."
> "I am less than...."
> "She almost gave me a heart attack."
> "I never have enough money."
> "If I sit in a draft, I always catch cold."
> "George always gets the breaks and I get the dirty jobs."
> "Mary always knows just what to say and I always say the wrong thing."

Your creative activity sets about to achieve that data as a goal. Your world is the product of your subconscious mind based on the data and goals given it by the conscious mind.

Your subconscious mind, in conjunction with the nervous system, constitutes a creative activity that operates automatically to achieve goals and it is always at work. If you are consciously programming a goal into it, it will work toward that goal.

If the subconscious is not consciously given a specific goal, it will usually seek one which is the easiest to attain, based on past experience. The result is little or no change in your life. If you desire any kind of change in your life, the first step is to establish conscious goals; positive goals that you want to see in your life.

Consider the true story of a man whom we will call Bobby. He is serving a life sentence in a mid-western prison as an incorrigible criminal. Bobby has spent more than half of his life behind bars and by his own admission is a success. When he was seventeen years old, he made a conscious decision to become the very best burglar in the business. He was a total success. He used very sophisticated equipment and in his last "job" made twenty-five thousand dollars for just one night's work. Now that he is in jail, he is considered by his peers to be the final authority on any question about burglaries. Bobby said, "Anyone can attain any goal they set for themselves. Look at me, I'm a perfect example of it. The mistake I made was setting a stupid goal."

What kind of goals have you set? If your answer to that question is "none," or "I don't know," there is another question to ask yourself: "What do I think about most of the time?" Now, if your answer to that question is inconsistent with what your life has been, you are kidding yourself. Your predominant thought-habits and patterns of the past have brought you to the place and circumstance in which you find yourself today. Today's thoughts are even now forming your tomorrow. When you do not set specific and conscious goals, that which you think about most of the time becomes your goal or goals. And you are always a success even if you are succeeding at being a failure.

You are a fantastically creative being right now. This is how you were created, and you can literally achieve anything of which you can conceive. Don't sell yourself short! You are not the product of a broken home, a devastated economy, a world in the upheaval of war, a minority group, a family of drunkards, or a poverty ridden neighborhood. You are the product of your own thinking processes. And whatever you are thinking about today is the cornerstone of your tomorrow. Right now, you have within you the innate ability to create the kind of life you want for "you." This is simply the way your Creator created you! You are really awesomely and wonderfully made!

IV

The Created You

GIVEN THE OPPORTUNITY, almost any adult can tell you how he came to be the person he is, and how he managed to accumulate the worldly goods he possesses. He will most likely tell you how he was affected either positively or negatively by his early family life, his racial or ethnic background, his early economic status, the economy of the nation, his physical stature or any other factor of which he can think. Now, as discussed in Chapter I, these factors did not directly affect him. Rather it was his reaction or response to them that affected his life. And once beyond childhood, those were *chosen* responses. Perhaps not consciously chosen, but chosen none the less.

Why would anyone choose a response that was contrary to one's own good? The answer is two-fold. First, the choice was made out of habit from an old mental frame of reference that may never have been or is not now valid. And secondly, the choice was the best choice that person could have made according to his emotional state and his intellectual understanding at that time. In short, he did the best he could at that specific point in time.

There is a major factor that plays a vital role in the kinds of response you choose either consciously or subconsciously. That factor is the mental picture that you have of yourself. This is your "self image." It is how you see "you" and how you feel about "you." Whether that mental picture is valid or invalid, it is the primary key to the level of life you are living and the circumstances in which you now find yourself. Your life and your circumstances are *always* consistent with your mental image of "you." If your self-image is one of overweight and unattractiveness, no amount of dieting and trips to a beauty salon will bring about a permanent change. If your image of "you" is unworthy of financial success, no amount of hard work or luck will change your financial status.

Changing your life or your world does not begin with manipulating and working to bring about change in the outer world. It is an "inside job." Changing your life begins with changing your image of *YOU* and your image of your place in the world. Your image of "you" has brought you to the place in life where you are right now and it will continue to do so unerringly. If you want change in your life, change your mental picture of "you." Your self-image can be changed, but only *you* can change it. Remember the "buck stops here!"

IMAGE INVENTORY

In order to effectively change your self-image, it is important to find out what your image is now and what areas need to be improved. It is kind of like having an automobile with an automatic transmission that doesn't shift properly. There is no need to overhaul the transmission if the problem is in the carburetor.

Make a personal inventory. Get two sheets of paper and a pen or pencil. *Stop* reading now and get the paper and pen.

Write down your opinion of "you." Describe yourself as you see "you," not as you think others see you. Be completely honest with yourself. Don't pull any punches. This is your personal inventory of "you" and it is no one's business but yours. Share it with no one, not even your spouse, parent, or best friend. Once again, stop reading and write out your inventory.

Now, if this inventory has been honestly done, the areas that need to be changed and improved upon will be quite obvious. You have made a personal diagnosis; now it's time to go to work making the needed changes.

On a separate piece of paper, write down how you would like to see "you." Once again, be honest and place no limitations on yourself. Be specific. Go into detail and write it all down. Stop reading now and write on the second sheet of paper how you would like to see "you."

This is *your* image goal and it is your business only. Don't share it with anyone, but make a practice of carrying it with you. Read it to yourself two or three times a day. Imagine yourself being what you have described. Read over your first personal inventory, make a mental note of the areas you wish to change and destroy the inventory. Tear it up into small pieces and throw it away. From this point forward, it is no longer a part of you.

The story is told of an eight-year-old English boy who wanted to be the Prime Minister of England. He played at it, he imagined himself as the Prime Minister and even had his picture taken as a school boy standing in front of Number Ten Downing Street. This was not only his goal but he saw himself as Prime Minister of England. His name was Harold Wilson.

There was another young man who imagined himself as the greatest prize fighter in the world. He ruffled some feathers and made himself unpopular in some circles but he never let go of his goal to be the "greatest." He often said, "I am the greatest." In the face of great adversity and every kind of religious, political, and ethnic stumbling block imaginable, he went on to become the greatest heavyweight boxer of his time. In the minds of many experts, he became the greatest boxer of the century. He truly became what he imaged himself to be — "the greatest."

"As a man thinketh in his heart, so is he."

The whole concept of your being a reflection or expression of the image you hold of "you" is not a new idea, nor is it the invention of those who have professionally explored it or have written books about it. It is simply the way your Creator created you, and you cannot change that. You can, through the conscious discipline of your thinking, change the product, but the *process* remains the same. You are the product of what you think.

In succeeding chapters, we will be discussing *how* to respond creatively and bring about changes in specific areas of your life, such as: love, conflicts, hurt feelings, criticism, health, and prosperity. Yet, in every instance, the ultimate goal is to create an all round, balanced, positive self-image that will create the kind of world you desire.

Remember:

You are worthy!

You are successful!

You are capable!

You are a unique creature of God that needs only measure up to the highest in you.

You can be what and who you choose to be!

You can choose to respond creatively to your world and have a new life and environment.

V

Using Creative Tools

THE NEXT LOGICAL STEP in learning to respond creatively and to effectively plant positive and worthy goals to be achieved, is to learn how you use your innate ability to create. How can you most effectively change what you think and what you think about? How can you get your goal-achieving subconscious mind going in the right direction? The obvious answer is "discipline." Discipline your thinking. Well, that is true but it is almost a non-answer unless you can come up with some specific and workable techniques.

Remember: The conscious mind sets the goals, makes the value judgments, but it must also keep the goal uppermost in the thought pattern. The subconscious mind accepts whatever the conscious mind gives it as *truth* without question and achieves whatever goals are put before it. The goal that is implanted time after time will get the action, just as the squeaky wheel gets the grease. You must let each phase of mind do the job it was created to do. Do not use the conscious mind to try to find the way or achieve the goal. That is the job of the subconscious. Your conscious mind chooses the goal or goals, holds to the goal consciously and the subconscious provides the "how to." You hold the goal, and the creative activity of your subconscious will give you the idea and lead you into the experiences needful to attain your goal. It is like using a computer: you punch in the problem and let the computer solve it. When working with a computer, you wouldn't periodically stop its problem-solving procedure in order to tell it what you found from experience won't work. No! You let *it* solve the problem. Your subconscious has infinitely more information stored away in it than you can consciously recall. Let the subconscious mind do its work and you, with your conscious mind, do yours.

IMAGINATION

One of the most powerful facets of your mind is your ability to imagine things. Used creatively, your imagination can change your life. What you are today and what you have in your life today, is the result of what you have imaged in the past. It is very probable that the imaging you were using in the past was not being creatively and consciously directed by you. This is where the "discipline" must come into play. In order to bring about change in your life, you must begin to decide consciously and creatively what you are going to image!

Some years ago a group of university students participated in a controlled experiment to test their power of imagination. The students were put into three groups. Each group was tested to find how accurate it was in making baskets from the free-throw line of a regulation basketball court. After initial testing, the first group was instructed to come back each day and practice making baskets in the same manner as they were tested. Each member of the group practiced for the same specified period of time each day. The second group, like the other groups, was not told why they were being tested, and they simply were released with no further instructions. This was the control group. After the first testing, the third group was instructed to practice throwing baskets in their imagination only, for the same period of time each day that group number one was actually practicing with a ball on a court. About three weeks later all three groups were retested for accuracy on the basketball court. Group number one (those who actually practiced) was twenty-four percent more accurate. Group number two (those who did nothing) had little or no change in their average. Groups number three (those who practiced in their imagination) was twenty-three percent more accurate.

A sixth grade teacher in a small town in western Oregon introduced this imaging concept to one of her classes. Each student decided on a specific goal and began imaging that goal as complete. They were instructed to visualize the goal only, not *how* the goal was to be attained. In the teacher's words, "I just can't begin to tell you in words how wonderful this has been. Some of the goals set that have had some very positive results have been, so far:

1. A girl now has fingernails to take care of instead of ones bitten down to the quick.
2. A boy scores higher in basket-ball than ever before.
3. A boy's handwriting is readable, whereas it used to be hardly legible.
4. A boy is turning in much higher quality work and getting better grades.
5. Another boy is friendlier and easier to get along with than he has been in the past.

These are just a few examples. There are actually many more."

Your imagination is powerful! Use it creatively to build your life the way you want your life to be.

Your subconscious mind directs your nervous system, yet it cannot distinguish between an actual event and an event that is vividly imagined in the conscious mind. If you imagine that there is a prowler sneaking around your backyard, in the garage, or downstairs rummaging through your valuables, the adrenalin is going to flow, your heart will beat faster and all of your physical senses will become more sensitive just as if there really were a prowler. Your subconscious and your nervous system respond to what you imagine or believe to be true; not necessarily what is actually true.

Set aside fifteen or twenty minutes two times each day to imagine consciously what you want. In the beginning stay with one or two specific goals that you believe are attainable. Vividly imagine yourself achieving the goal. Do not get involved with the "how to."

Center your imagination on the completed goal and how you would benefit and be involved with the end product.

If it is a new car that you desire, then in your imagination see the car you want. Get in and "start" the engine. "Feel" the upholstery, "smell" that new car odor. In short, experience having the car in your imagination. The more detailed and involved you can get in your imagination, the more effectively you will attain the goal. God gave you your imagination, and it is yours to help you have what you want in life. USE IT! Use it consciously! And use it creatively for your good.

WHAT ARE YOU THINKING?

We are the products of our thinking. Yet, too much of the time we think about things we don't want and pay little attention to our own thought processes. We are thinking all the time, yet most of the time we don't think about what we are thinking, or at the very least, we don't consider what the consequences will be of that thinking.

A good example of this kind of thinking is "worrying." Most worrying is destructive thinking, or at best non-productive thinking. By definition, to worry is to go over and over in one's mind the thoughts and ideas about a subject or circumstance. When you worry, it is usually over something you are anxious about; something you fear. So in your mind, you go over all of the "what ifs." "What if I can't pay the bill?"

"What if the store calls my employer?" "What if they repossess the television set?" "What if I lose my job?" All of these "what ifs" of a negative nature serve only to reinforce or hasten to completion an old negative goal. Remember, you are what you think about. With not too much mental discipline, you can change those negative "what ifs" to positive ones. "What if I get a better job?" "What if I could pay all the bills?" The positive "what ifs" reinforce and hasten to completion your positive goals. In effect, positive worry. If you want to keep something or some condition in your life—worry about it.

Look back in your life. Did negative worry *ever* help you solve a problem?

People don't normally make a conscious effort to worry negatively. They simply respond to a circumstance out of old thinking habits and the worrying begins. Those thinking and responding habits can be changed, but only you can change them in you. Become aware of what you are thinking about.

Here is a technique for becoming more consciously aware of what you are thinking about on a day-by-day basis. On three inch by five inch white cards, write or print in bold letters, "DO YOU WANT IT, _____?" In the blank space write your name. Put the cards in various places where you will see them often—places like above the kitchen sink, on the bathroom mirror, on the night stand next to the alarm clock, on the refrigerator door, in the top of your briefcase, under the glass of your desk, or anywhere in your work area and perhaps on the dashboard of your car. Each time you see one of the cards, let it remind you to examine what you are thinking at that moment. If you are thinking about something you desire, keep it up. If you find you are thinking about something you do not want—change what you are thinking about to something that is creative and for your good.

The advice given to us almost two thousand years ago still stands valid: "Whatsoever things are of good report, if there be any virtue, and if there be any praise, think on these things."

VI

Goals

IN THE PRECEDING CHAPTER, goals and the mechanics of how goals are achieved, were discussed in a general way. In this chapter techniques will be applied to specific kinds of goals.

Generally speaking, goals can be separated into two basic categories, long-term and short-term.

Long-term goals are usually more general in nature than short-term goals. As an example, a young person in high school or college might have a long-term goal to be a surgeon, specializing in heart surgery. The specifics of that goal will be far less defined than the multitude of short-term goals that will be established and achieved as he works toward the goal of "heart surgeon." As that once long-term goal gets closer, it will become a short-term goal and be more and more specifically defined. If this young person is going to be a successful human being, a new long-term goal will have to be established. There should always be a goal that is being sought, something to look forward to.

Just as valid a long-term goal might be for a young

girl to get married, have a nice home, a loving husband, and five beautiful children. Or she might want to become president of a bank. Either is a valid goal which began as a long-term goal with many specific short-term goals along the way.

Goals, especially the longer term goals, should not be rigid or unchangeable. Specific — yes, but rigid — no! As we grow and unfold in consciousness and in awareness of our world, our values and desires change right along with our growth. It is perfectly valid to change a long-term goal if it can be seen that an alternative goal is more desirable.

Shakespeare said, "To thine own self be true," and that is good advice. One important part of being true to one's self is accepting the inevitable inconsistencies of self — the seeming inconsistencies that come along with intellectual, physical, and spiritual growth.

It has been said that man does not live by bread alone — he must have peanut butter as well. And there may have been a time in your life when peanut butter was your favorite food. Is it now? There may have been a time when your favorite pastime was reading comic books, or acting in a school play, or playing with toy soldiers, or sewing, or any number of things that have long since ceased to be an important part of your life. Accept the changes that take place in you, for they are evidence of your growth and unfoldment. You are *never* too old to grow some more. Bend and let the winds of time caress you as you move toward the life of fulfillment. The only consistent element in your life is change. Move with it and be a part of it.

The short-term goals are the goals that you work with on a day-to-day basis. They are the goals that shape your life and lead you to that long-term goal. Short-term goals should be as specific as possible and directed toward such things as attitudes, vocations, personal relationships, prosperity, health, and peace of mind. (Prosperity and Health are covered in separate chapters.)

The first step in setting short-term goals is to establish your list of priorities. Write out the list in order of your priorities at this time. (Stop right now and write out your order of priorities. There is no time like the present and changes will not take place until *you* do something. The "buck" stops with you and your "world" starts with you.) At least once a week this priority list should be reviewed. If a priority needs to be re-evaluated or a goal has been achieved, or if you have just changed your mind about a goal, rewrite the list according to *your* priority at this time. *Important* —Review the list at least once a week.

Consciously work on only one or two goals at a time. It is possible and effective to combine one or two or even three goals into one "imaging" time. In this manner you might be effectively working on as many as four or five at a time. Through the exercise of reading the list, you will be "working" subconsciously on all of the goals.

Pick two times a day that are convenient to you; when you can be quiet, and retreat into your imagination for fifteen minutes. The most effective times are early in the morning and just before you retire in the evening. The evening is especially effective, even if you fall asleep during your imaging time. Remember: Your goal-achieving activity is at work all the time — even when you are asleep. Give yourself two fifteen-minute periods each day to help you build a better tomorrow.

As you begin to imagine your goal, *do not* say to yourself, "This is the way it will be tomorrow or next week or next month." Do not set time limits, maximum or minimum. Say to yourself, "For the next fifteen minutes I am going to imagine myself _____." Imagine yourself as having achieved the goal, enjoy it, feel it, be a part of it, and relax into it. Do not try to imagine the "how to" part. That is the job of the subconscious with its varied and vast resources. Your conscious job is to image the end product only. One note of caution: Don't tell anyone what you are doing. Don't advertise!

The following are some specific applications to a variety of situations and goals. The variations on these are as endless as individual needs might dictate.

THE OFFICE CONFLICT

If there is someone with whom you work or with whom you have regular contact and you have difficulty dealing with this person or simply can't seem to get along with him, use the imaging process. In your mind's eye see yourself and that person (or group of people) going about your normal duties *without* friction. Pick the kinds of circumstances that usually cause the most friction and see both of you working together in complete cooperation. Try to bring as much detail into your imaging as possible. Do not try to work out how you arrived at the point of cooperation, only visualize the end result.

THE DUTY FAMILY GATHERING

From time to time everyone has to go to a "duty" social gathering. More than likely it is a family gathering, but it could be a business-social gathering. In any event, the train of thought preceding the event goes something like this, "What a bore, you know what will happen. Uncle Charlie will get loaded and Aunt Minnie will dominate the conversation, talking about how sick she is." Don't spend your time prior to the event stewing about what a bad time you will have. Instead, image what it would be like if Uncle Charlie stayed sober and Aunt Minnie was a delight to be around. Once again, image what you *want*. See the final product.

A NEW JOB

If you are seeking a new job, decide specifically what you want to do and get all the information you can about the position and the company or companies that do the job. See yourself successfully functioning in the desired position. In your imaging time become that functioning employee. Don't try to rationalize how you got there, just be there in your imagination.

If there is a testing program as part of the pre-employment process, go through the testing in your imagination and think what it would be like to get the highest score in the company's history. Use your imagination and get involved with what you are imaging.

THE NEW HOUSE

Decide specifically what you want and where you want it. If you can find a picture of what you want, put it where you see it every day. In your imaging time see the house, see what color it is, walk through the yard, go into the house and put you and your family in it. During that imaging period of time—move in. And again, don't try to rationalize how you found the house or how you came up with the down payment. Imagine the end product only.

BEING SLIM AND TRIM

Most people weigh more than they should, and most overweight people give a lot of thought to diet. The medical profession is becoming more and more convinced that weight loss is not permanent unless the self-image is changed. If you want to lose weight, your first step is to stop saying that you want to or are going to lose weight. Because you are probably an optimist basically, you know that you usually find things that you lose. Make up your mind to "get rid" of weight rather than to "lose" it.

There is a popular fad that many people think is effective. It consists of putting a grossly fat caricature of a person or a picture of a huge pig on the refrigerator door, the idea being that it reminds you not to eat so much. Yet, it actually intensifies the concept of *fat* and keeps impressing the subconscious with an image of fat. It reminds you of precisely what you don't want. A far better idea is to cut out a picture of a person of the weight you desire, put a snapshot of your face on the picture and put that picture on the refrigerator door. Image what you want!

When you go shopping for clothes, usually a good portion of your time is spent in looking just for the enjoyment of looking. Do your looking, just for the joy of looking, in the size you plan to attain, not in the size you are now wearing.

In your imaging times see yourself slim and trim, wearing the kinds of clothes you would like to be wearing, and doing the kinds of things you would enjoy doing. Let your imaging be vivid, in detail, inventive and even fun. Think thin and establish a thin image of yourself.

Many medical and psychological authorities are convinced that the brain monitors the amount of fat in the body and determines how efficient it will be in using up calories according to a pre-set ideal. It is important that this pre-set ideal gets changed, because it is a part of the self-image. Regardless of how overweight you have been or how overweight your family has been or is, you can change your image of you and bring that weight down.

When you are using any of these techniques, do not tell anyone what you are doing. There are bound to be some doubts in your own mind and that is okay, but you do not need to have your "friends" (especially the over-weight ones) telling you that it won't work. And they will be able to come up with all kinds of excuses and rationalizations. You will be dealing with your own old thought habits and they are plenty to handle. Keep your own counsel and do your own work.

RESERVE JUDGMENT

Whether you are using the imaging technique for weight control or any other goal you choose, do not make a value judgment on its effectiveness for three weeks. Science has established this lapse of time as a kind of reconstruction period for the automatic subconscious responses to take control. For example, after an amputation it takes about three weeks for phantom pain and feeling to disappear. If you move into a new house or apartment, it usually takes about three weeks for you to respond automatically to the locations of light switches and to the differently arranged cupboards and drawers. Relax and give yourself the opportunity to change.

So often, we human beings try too hard during the first few days or weeks when we are working on a habit-change. It is impatience with ourselves that causes a degree of frustration. We seem to be much like the aborigine who saved and saved from his meager wages so he could buy a very special custom-made boomerang. After several years of frugal living and saving, the big day came and he purchased the finely balanced, perfectly molded boomerang. Then he spent the rest of his life trying to throw away his old boomerang.

We are not much different. We keep trying to cast away old habits, old hurts, and old ways of doing things. Yet, more often than not, the solution to many of our problems is similar to that of the aborigine. We don't have to cast them away or struggle to rid ourselves of them. All we have to do is put them down and walk away.

Do your work in the realm of mind and imagination, and *let* the changes come, instead of trying to *make* the changes come.

VII

Creative Habits

ALMOST EVERYONE has some habit he would like to break and almost everyone has a sure-fire way of breaking almost any kind of habit. It would seem that most of the habit-breaking techniques deal basically with the outer manifestation of the habit rather than the inner response that triggers the outer action. A good example is the use of a chemical applied to the fingernails that tastes bad so one will stop biting their fingernails, or taking a chemical internally that makes a cigarette taste bad, or makes one ill when he smokes. Many techniques employ the use of sheer will power. These concepts do not take into consideration how the habit was acquired. Habits are not generally the result of a physical trauma or discomfort, nor are habits formed by will power, and the habits are not formed over night.

Habits are like callouses on our hands and feet; they develop over a period of time until one day we wake up to the fact that we have a habit. They are usually responses to a signal-pattern in the subconscious mind. It is very much like responding to the ringing telephone. Our response is automatic. We respond to signals all the time. Our first response in the morning may be to the alarm clock ringing. We respond to hunger. Very quickly our hand will move away from a flame in response to a heat signal. One may reach for a cigarette automatically when a cup of coffee is served. Again, responding to a signal from the subconscious.

Many of our automatic responses to subconscious signals are beneficial and even vital to our well-being. In a sense, they are good habits — very good habit-responses. There are many subconscious signals that we answer out of habit that are detrimental to our health, happiness, appearance, or well-being. These are the habits we want to change. The usual term we would use is "break" the habit of responding. Too often as we try to "break" a habit through will power, we just reinforce it in the subconscious.

A very good way to "break" a habit is not to try to "break" it in its outer manifestation. Instead, employ the imaging technique.

FINGERNAIL BITING

This approach is especially effective for women. As you work in your imagination, see your fingernails long, shape them, file and buff them, polish them, lightly scratch yourself with them. Imagine as vividly and in as much detail as possible. Enjoy having long fingernails. Admire them, but do not try to imagine how you stopped biting them. Just image the end product.

SMOKING

If you really desire to stop smoking, use the imaging technique. Image yourself not smoking at the time that you most like to smoke. Vividly see yourself not smoking while others around you are smoking and there are cigarettes lying on the table. Imagine yourself enjoying not smoking. Spend about fifteen minutes twice a day in this manner.

DELAYING ACTION

To supplement your imaging program, practice delaying your responses to signals coming from your subconscious mind. When the signal comes to light up a cigarette with a cup of coffee, put off responding until you begin your second cup. Use any excuse or time-frame to put off responding. Remember—you are in control of your responses. You don't have to answer that subconscious signal any more than you *have* to answer the telephone or the ringing doorbell. In the beginning, put off answering; play a delaying game.

When I was a young police officer in a large western city, my first partner and training officer was a man with over twenty years' experience. As the saying goes, he was very "street wise" and he had his own proven code of operation that he called "Russell's Law." One of the cardinal rules in "Russell's Law" dealt with where and how a police officer sat in a restaurant. An officer always sat away from the door, back to a wall and facing the cash register. This rule was backed up with some violent tales of what had happened to officers, including himself, who had been foolish enough to violate this rule. He told stories about everything from an officer being pistol whipped with his own service revolver, which had been taken away from him by the hold-up man, to the embarrassment of having a restaurant robbed while the officers were dining with their backs to the door. I learned the lesson well and as the years passed, I formed a strong habit, and during those years as a policeman it was a good habit that had been proven valid. The only problem came up when I was out socially with other people and simply could not sit with my back to the room in a restaurant. This caused a little inconvenience, but friends understood and I always got to sit with my back against the wall.

After about six years of this training, I left the police department but the habit-response stayed with me for years. This was a signal or a bell that I had to learn *not* to answer. I began by putting off a response and rationalizing with myself that I was no longer carrying a gun and no one was going to single me out of the crowd and rap me on the head. I put off responding just a few moments at a time—until the waiter brought the menu; then, until I had read the menu, or any other delaying tactic I could find. Sometimes it didn't work for very long, and I would have to ask someone to change places with me, but I kept working at it. While I was sitting there putting off responding, I would consciously try to relax, get involved in a conversation, anything to keep me from answering the signal. It took a while but finally I built a *new* habit of *not* responding.

The most effective way to "break" a habit is to form a *new* habit of *not* responding. This is creative responsibility, or responding in a creatively different way.

We all have many signals to which we respond, and these signals are habits, even though they do not seem like habits. From childhood we accept certain concepts from our parents and peers that may or may not be valid for us! We accept these opinions and respond to them as if they were true. Many times we go on for years responding from a subconscious signal that is inconsistent with what we want in life. Some of the obvious things and people to which we respond out of habit are employers, credit managers, relatives, in-laws, policemen, crowds, high places, closed-in places, being alone, being in the dark, or strangers. It is good to examine honestly how we react to the signals certain people or situations trigger. Logically examine the circumstances, and then practice delaying the response, and if applicable, use the imaging process.

If you know you have an appointment with a credit manager or your employer, and you feel a sense of anxiety, then use your imaging technique. See that person as just a person with the same kinds of signals within him to which he is responding. The credit manager wants to be helpful. After all he is in the business of lending money or extending credit, and you are just as important to him as he is to you. Image your meeting as a total success, attaining the goals you have set. Win, lose, or draw in the meeting itself, that long period before the meeting will be spent free of anxiety and negative worry.

Check to be aware of your automatic responses. They are response-habits. If you respond in ways that turn people off, bring out their hostility, or put them on the defensive, take a close look at *you!* You may very well be responding out of habit to a belief or opinion that is no longer really valid for you.

Your mind has a fantastic ability to adapt, to change, and to create a new life for you. Use it!

VIII

Creating Through Conflict

IN VIRTUALLY EVERY human problem, when all outer trappings are stripped away, there is always one basic element present. That basic element is conflict. Let's understand this word *conflict*. So often *conflict* is thought of in terms of war, physical combat, or deep difficult struggle. Yet, in the final analysis, it is simply two or more points of view that are not compatible. A conflict is a difference of opinion. In human relations it always takes two to have a conflict. The old song said that it takes two to tango, and it is just as true to say that it takes two to tangle.

Mature adults can resolve virtually any conflict if they choose to do so. Any conflict can be resolved if the effort is directed toward *resolving* the conflict rather than attaining the advantage. When a conflict comes to light between individuals or groups of individuals, each side begins to jockey for a position of advantage or control. This can be observed in marital conflicts, labor conflicts, neighborhood conflicts, or international conflicts. It always seems that the basic conflict (difference of opinion) gets lost in the struggle for advantage.

Whenever you find yourself involved in a conflict, always strive to keep your cool and attempt to resolve the conflict. Do not let your desire to gain advantage be your motive.

The conflicts that seem to cause the greatest anguish are those that arise within the home or in close personal relationships. These can be dealt with quite effectively, provided two elements are present. First, that both (or all) parties agree that each individual's opinion is valid from the holder's frame of reference. Second, that both (or all) parties desire to resolve the conflict.

BRAINSTORMING A COMPROMISE

The conflicts (differences of opinion) in close personal relationships that cause divorces, broken friendships, estranged families, and rebellious children are usually relatively minor. If these conflicts are dealt with intelligently and individually in their early stages rather than being allowed to accumulate and fester out of true perspective, they can be readily solved. When lifted out of emotional turmoil and viewed with a degree of objectivity, it can be seen that these conflicts run the gamut from things like: the children's bed time, how to shop in the super-market, how to spend the vacation, or what television program to view; to the discipline of the children, the wife's role in the family structure, or the husband's role. Between the poles of conflict, there is always room for a reasonable compromise, providing the question of gained advantage is put aside. It is important for all parties involved to realize that each party has formed his opinion based on past data stored in the subconscious mind as valid information. Hence, each opinion is valid from the holder's frame of reference, and this opinion should not be ridiculed by the opposition. Neither party should try to change or ridicule the opposition, but should *allow* each the liberty to change his mind without being informed, even by implication, "I told you so!"

An effective way to find workable compromises is by *brainstorming*. It is most effective when it can be made into a light game but is totally ineffective if either party is angry or feeling hurt.

Choose a time when there will be no interruptions for about an hour. You will need a pencil, paper, a smile, and a desire to *resolve* the conflict. Have each person write out his opinion in as few words as possible. This opinion should not include any reasons or rationalization—just the position or opinion. Then bounce back and forth every possible solution, no matter how ridiculous or far out it may seem. Write down all ideas brought forth. Let your imagination go free and see how many solutions can be written down.

Assume the conflict is over family television viewing:

Opinion number one: Viewing should be limited to the news and educational programs for the children.

Opinion number two: Viewing is recreational and there should be no limit for the children.

Possible compromise:
1. Vote of the family
2. One hour of each kind of program a day
3. Allow the children to pick shows they want and have the parents choose from the list.
4. Everyone must watch the 6:00 P.M. News
5. Buy another television set
6. Get one set for each person (make them coin operated).
7. Get rid of the television set
8. Get rid of the children
9. Get rid of the parents

Let the list grow until you feel that everyone concerned has had a voice and hopefully some fun. Now go back over the list and cross out the suggestions with which no one really agrees and begin to refine, sort out and combine others until two or more possible and workable compromises are reached. Don't make a decision at this point, but don't discuss it any more either—sleep on it! On the following day, review the possibilities and put one into effect on a trial basis. Remember, nothing is permanent and there is always room for future compromise. Change is the orderly flow of life—let it happen.

CHANGING MASKS

From time to time in everyone's experience, there comes a conflict that seems beyond resolving because the "other person" (and it always seems to be the "other person") is unwilling, uncaring, or incapable of trying to resolve it. In this instance, we usually just learn to live with it because we can't change another person. It is true that we can't change another, but we can help them to change themselves.

As discussed before, your life is a constant chain of responses. From the moment you are born until the instant you die, your waking hours are spent responding to people, things, and circumstances in your outer world or to the thoughts of your own mind. All of those people in the world about you are no different; they too are responding.

If you were asked to identify one aspect of another person that either attracted you or repelled you, the word would most likely be "personality." This word "personality" comes from the root word "persona" which means "mask." Generally speaking, you wear a mask that reflects what you think about yourself, your peers, your world, and your basic ethical standards. However, all day long, over this basic mask you have a wide collection of masks that you put on and take off at will or without thinking.

For example, picture an ordinary man, in an ordinary neighborhood, walking his dog around the block. As he leaves his own yard, he waves a friendly hand to his next-door neighbor whom he happens to like (Good Neighbor Mask). A few doors down the block he meets Mr. Manybucks who owns half of the town, and they pass the time of day (Make a Good Impression Mask). Down around the corner, Joe Sloppy tries to borrow ten dollars until Friday (Get

Lost Mask, or perhaps, I'm Broke Too Mask). Around the next corner, Miss Dixie Delight is soaking up the warm sunshine, clad in a very brief bikini (Dashing Man of the World Mask). Often this mask is accompanied by an unconscious straightening of the shoulders and tucking in of the tummy.

Sometimes a "mask" is consciously put on to bring out a specific kind of response. A parent might put on an "angry mask" when disciplining a child. The most effective "mask" is obviously the one which is honest and proceeds forth naturally from the subconscious. Most astute adults can see past a "put on mask."

Whenever you change a "mask," whether it is a subtle, real change from within, or a dramatic, obvious one, those people who are responding to you must respond to your "mask." When your mask is changed, others have no choice but to change their responses.

You can change your mask in a very subtle, positive creative manner from within by consciously and repeatedly changing how you think about someone. The usual pattern is to stew and fret about what the other person is doing and to imagine how his actions and attitudes will affect you. This process only serves to build up resentment (and possibly hate) in you. Your resentment is passed on by your "mask" and picked up consciously and/or subconsciously by the other person. A vicious circle is established and constructive communication ceases. In addition, any resentment or hate held by you hurts *only* you. For your own sake, learn to let go of resentment and hate. It is self-destructive.

Commit the following three statements to memory and go over and over them in your mind (or out loud when you are by yourself) whenever you find yourself thinking about the offending person.

> I love you __(name)__ .
> I bless you.
> I let you go

Do this over and over whenever the person comes to mind, until something else comes to mind that is unrelated. It is important that the person *does not* know that you are playing this mental game in your own mind. It is also important to understand what you are saying and why these specific words are used.

The first statement, "I love you _____," has nothing to do with affection or even liking the other person. The word "love" is used in its purest sense, in the manner that God loves or as you might "love" mankind or as a mother might love a child who is misbehaving (love is discussed at length in Chapter X). The important point is to generate the *idea* of "love" in your mind in order to replace the thoughts of resentment. In this instance you are loving for *your* good and its effect on you.

To bless someone means to "pronounce holy" or "one with God." Each and every person, regardless of your opinion of him or his actions, is a product of the same Creator and the Creator indwells all creation. So, let go and do not carry his burden as well as your own.

A young school teacher, in her first teaching assignment, was about to resign because of one little boy in her class. She simply could not cope with him and his antics, which disrupted the entire class. The harder she tried to control him with all the techniques she had learned, the more difficult he became. After hearing this "I love you, I bless you, I let you go" technique explained, she tried it. Within three weeks the boy had changed completely. He was helpful, well mannered, and a positive addition to the class. The boy, like most children, was very receptive to his teacher's inner attitude being reflected in her "mask." Instead of reading resentment, uncertainty, anger, and anxiety in the teacher's "mask," he began reading *love* and had no choice but to change his response.

People respond to whatever "mask" you show. Change the "mask" and they have no choice but to change their response.

IX

Creating Out of Hurt

RARE IS THE PERSON who has never had hurt feelings. We can all say that we have been hurt by someone at sometime. Yet, in reality no one has the power to hurt us unless we give them that power. It would be much truer to say that we hurt ourselves by our own response to the words or actions of others.

Dr. Benet Wong, a Vancouver, British Columbia, psychiatrist tells a story about himself. "I remember when I was younger. I could never understand why all the other kids always wanted to call me 'Chink'. Everywhere I went, they called 'chinky, chinky, Chinaman', and all the other things, and it hurt. Each time the word was said, it was like a knife stabbing me in the chest. There was a deep hurt, which I never did understand because the word seemed pretty respectable. I wrote down the word and I analyzed the word. I looked at the letters, and they were all the same letters in the alphabet that you spell 'ink' with, and all sorts of other things which seemed pretty innocuous. But every time they uttered 'chink', it was like a stab wound in my chest."

"It wasn't until later," Dr. Wong continued, "that I discovered that the word 'chink' was just the word 'chink' and that's all it was. What was happening, was that people were offering me the word 'chink' as though it were a knife. I was taking the knife out of people's hands, stabbing myself with it and saying, 'Why do you hurt me so much?'"

People offer us knives all day long. Sometimes we stab ourselves and are hurt. More often we use the knives to cut ourselves down or cut ourselves off from our good. We look about ourselves and make judgments that these people are "thick skinned" and those are "thin skinned" according to how they handle the knives handed to them. Then we rate ourselves somewhere along the scale between thin and thick skinned and hurt accordingly. The fact that one person may not be easily hurt does not mean that he is callous or insensitive; it simply indicates that he has learned to deal with hurt feelings and most likely has a strong, positive image of himself. The person whose feelings are hurt easily has a poor self-image.

Hurt feelings can be creatively and effectively dealt with in two ways. The first and most apparent, is for *you* to improve your own self-image as discussed in Chapter IV. The second, and equally important way to deal with hurt feelings, is to understand what actually causes hurt feelings. What goes into the make-up of the "knife" of which Dr. Wong spoke?

Hurt feelings are caused by one thing, and all hurt feelings have this element no matter how deeply it is hidden. The element is criticism. The criticism may be directed or implied, but it is the basis for the response of hurt feelings. In a very true sense, criticism is the "knife."

A direct criticism would be a statement directed to you saying, "Your hair looks funny combed in that manner," or "Your clothes are too gaudy and out of style."

An indirect criticism sometimes must be ferreted out of the feelings and actions expressed by another person. If a man leaves his wife of ten years for another woman, the wife will most likely be hurt. The criticism here is indirect but criticism none the less. Indirectly and through his actions, the husband is saying to his wife, "This woman is more worthy of me than you are," or that the wife in some way is less than the new girl friend. Criticism is the "knife" but it is also the key to dealing with the hurt feelings. To try to deal directly with the hurt feelings is to work with the symptom rather than what caused the symptom. You can learn to respond creatively to criticism if you so choose. The choice of response is totally yours. You can choose to be hurt and be miserable, or you can grow into that happy image that is your goal.

Whenever you feel that stab of hurt, let it be a signal to you that you have accepted a criticism. Stop! Ferret out and ascertain in your own mind what the criticism is specifically. Then always ask yourself one question about the criticism, "From *my* frame of reference, is this criticism valid?" Answer the question within yourself as honestly and bluntly as you are able. This questioning is an inner activity that need not be shared with anyone at any time. You are a competent human being with just as many valid opinions from your frame of reference as the next person. Judge the criticism honestly and fairly from *your* frame of reference only. If you determine that the criticism is valid, then accept it as constructive criticism. Get busy and do something about changing you.

In the event that you determine from your point of view the criticism is *not* valid, let it go! It is the one who criticized you who has a problem to deal with — not you! There is no need for you to be burdened or hurt by his or her opinion. Everyone is entitled to his opinion and that goes equally for you as well. If Jesus, Buddha, or anyone of the great prophets of history were to return and walk among us today, there would be plenty of people ready and eager to criticize them too.

Criticism can be your friend or your foe. The choice is yours. There is no need for you to hurt. Examine those "knives" people hand you, but you don't have to stick them in yourself. It is just as easy to let them drop harmlessly into the dust. Declare, "I love you friend, I bless you, and I let you go. It is your problem, not mine."

There are those times in everyone's life that hurts occur and it seems that only time eases the pain. Yet, to hold onto the hurt and the other person involved, can only serve to prolong the hurt. Love them, bless them, and let go so you can regain your peace.

X

A Priceless Gift

"LOVE" IS PROBABLY the most popular word in our language, if not the favorite, certainly the "sentimental" favorite. Yet, it is one of the most misused words in our language. How often do you hear someone say, "I just love chocolate ice cream," or "I love to swim"? Stop and think! What on earth does chocolate ice cream or swimming have to do with love?

Countless words in books and articles have been written about love, not to mention the words in songs and poems. There is probably not a person living, who attends any church, synagogue, or temple, with any degree of regularity, who hasn't heard a lesson or sermon based on love. Love is a good, popular, and important subject—yet, a specific definition of love remains elusive.

A specific definition remains just beyond our grasp because love has many, many definitions. If you ask ten people to define the word, you will get ten different answers. If you go to the dictionary, you will find Mr. Webster to be just as ambiguous and just as indefinite. His list of definitions ranges from affection to a zero score in tennis.

It seems that perhaps the word "love" is not definitive enough by itself. Maybe we need to develop some new words in the English language for "love," so that we know exactly what we are talking about. We do this with many other words — so why not with "love"?

Let's consider the word *apple,* for example. If the word *apple* is mentioned to a group of people, each person visualizes a different kind of apple, and there are many. So we become more specific by using names according to specific varieties: Crab, Winesap, Jonathan, or Pippin — all apples, to be sure, but each with specific characteristics and uses.

So let's do the same thing with the word "love," and we don't have to invent any new words because they already exist in other languages. The Greeks have as good a separation as any. They have three kinds of "love," each with a specific application. These words are *philia, eros,* and *agape.*

Let's look at *philia* first. This is the love of friends; the kind of love that grows between friends because of a mutual rapport or through a common objective. In this kind of love we usually have to like the other person first, then the liking grows into love. All of us know this kind of love and we have all experienced it.

Now let's look at *eros. Eros* is the kind of love we find between a man and a woman. Here we find an ardent desire, a physical yearning. And this is the kind of love that usually comes to mind when we hear a man say that he loves his wife. *Eros* love is not all that love is; it is simply a kind of love.

Then we come to *agape* love. As defined in Webster's dictionary, agape love is, "Spontaneous self-giving love, expressed freely without calculation of cost or gain to the giver or merit on the part of the receiver." This is where we love, simply because it is our nature to love. This is how we love our children, even when they misbehave, hurt, or disappoint us — we love them. In *agape* love, it is not necessary to like — only to love.

Jesus said for us to *love* one another. He didn't say we had to like others, to like the way they act, or how they dress. Jesus said, "Love one another."

We have broken love down into three categories:

    Philia — love of friends, rapport.

    Eros — affection, physical love, as between a man and woman.

    Agape — spiritual: we love because it is our nature to love.

With apples we did the same thing, but we didn't define what an apple is. We can define or describe it as being a fruit that is round in shape, containing a fibrous core with seeds, surrounded by an edible meat, which in turn is covered by a skin. Now all kinds of apples, even if they have different uses or flavors, still have the same basic elements.

The same truth applies to love. There are different kinds of love but they all share the same basic elements.

Erich Fromm outlines these elements in his book, *The Art of Loving,* as care, responsibility, respect, and knowledge. And all four of these elements are interdependent on one another, so let's take a closer look at them.

First we have *care,* and care is very important because we can't love unless we care. We must care whether the object of our love is happy, nourished, warm. We must care about his well-being. Can you imagine loving your friend, your spouse, your fellow-man, or even your dog, and yet not caring if he is happy, hungry, or sick? Of course not!

Next we have *responsibility*—and it is an outgrowth of care. It is a voluntary act and means to be able and ready to respond. A person who cares or loves, responds to others, responds to another's needs, his joys, or his sadnesses. A parent responds to the cry of a child. A friend responds to the joys, hurts, and triumphs of his friends. And this leads us into the next element — respect.

Respect comes from the Latin word which means to look, (or more), to look back; to take another look and see the other person as he really is; to know that he has the same given potential in him that you do; yet, to see also his individuality and not judge him by your own standards; to allow him to unfold in *his* own way.

Respect is not possible without the fourth element, *knowledge* or understanding. It is necessary to *know* those whom we love, or to *understand* what they really are. People are outer expressions of their Creator and the power and love of their Creator is in them. When anyone, loved-one or complete stranger, acts in a way that seems to be wrong, unloving, angry, or whatever, look a bit deeper and try to understand. The act of anger is almost always just a facade. Look behind the anger and you will find any number of possible causes: fear, hurt feelings, embarrassment, physical pain, a feeling of ineptness or inferiority. Transcend the concern for yourself and try to see the other fellow in his own terms. Only in this way can you begin to understand him.

So there we have the basic elements of love: care, responsibility, respect, and knowledge. And all four of these elements are found in all three categories of love: *philia, eros,* and *agape.*

For a moment let's go back to the apples. We agree that different kinds of apples all share the same basic elements. Yet, there is something else we must take into consideration. What good is an apple if you just ignore it? So now we must find a common usage for all apples. The obvious common usage could be eating. We may prepare apples in countless ways: pie, applesauce, pickles, cider, or in salad, but we end up eating them. We have to take action and use the apples if they are to be of any benefit. If the apples just hang on the tree, they will drop off, wither, and rot away.

In a similar manner, we must come up with a common usage for all three kinds of love. We do have within us, all the love possible for a person to have, but if we don't use it, what good is it? First, we must remember that love is not passive. Love has been described as "an action, the practice of a human power." Love is an activity. To love, we must do something. So what one thing can we do that will fit all three kinds of love? We can *give* love!

Jesus said, "It is more blessed to give than to receive." And almost two thousand years later a foremost doctor of psychiatry, Erich Fromm, said, "Giving is more joyous than receiving, not because of the deprivation but because in the act of giving lies the expression of my aliveness."

So the common usage of all kinds of love is giving, not necessarily giving things, but giving the greatest of gifts—the real gifts—love, faith, understanding, care, responsibility, respect. And we give not with the idea that we will get something in return. We give—we love—because it is our nature to give—to love.

An apple is of no use until you eat it—and love is of no use until you give it.

The key word here is "give." Give love, don't barter, try to win, buy, sell, or even seek love. Give it!

Sometimes we wonder how we arrived at some of the misconceptions we have about love, and yet we hear the answer by just listening to ourselves and those around us. We have been taught by word and example from childhood:

"If you love Mommy, you'll eat your spinach."
"I love you when you act like that."
"I don't love you when you do that!"
"If you love me, you will stay home tonight."
"Mind Daddy or he won't love you."

The list is endless and really kind of ridiculous. Love is not a club or a tool. Love is a priceless gift freely given.

Any "love" relationship in which love is bartered or used for gain is doomed simply because sooner or later, one party in the relationship will decide that he is getting less than he is giving. Resentment from getting the short end of the trade begins to build and the relationship begins to crumble.

Often in counseling sessions, people cry out and ask, "What can I give? I've tried to give my loved-one everything he needs." The answer is, "Give them what *you* need." There is no way that you can crawl behind the mask of another human being and *know* what his needs really are. He shows you only what he wants to show and quite often only what he is able to show emotionally.

In an established personal relationship, you will be more apt to give the thing that is needed the most by giving what you need. If it is tenderness you need, give tenderness. If it is trust you need, then trust. And so on down the list of those intangibles we share with our fellow human beings. There is a bonus feature in this kind of giving. In every established religious and ethical philosophy, there is a common axiom — whatever you give, you receive:

Give love — love is returned
Give trust — you're trusted
Lie — you're lied to
Hate — you're hated

Rod McKuen said it all in fifteen short words, "I could have said that love at best is giving what you need to get." (*Stanyan Street & Other Sorrows;* Random House).

There is a special kind of light or radiance that we have all observed in certain people. It is difficult to describe, yet easy to recognize. We see "it" in the face of a mother as she tends her baby. We see "it" in a small child's upturned face or the young person enjoying life. We often see "it" in the elderly and sometimes we see "it" in a person who just seems to have "it." Each of these people is expressing one thing in common — love!

The mother loves her child just because she is the mother. No matter what the child's response is — the mother just loves. The small child loves because love is an innate part of his being. He knows nothing else. He hasn't been taught about fear, hate, or prejudice yet. He may not know it intellectually, but he is expressing the love that his Creator meant him to express. The young person, perhaps a teenager, is often carefree and swept up with the marvels of life. The fortunate ones never lose this zest for life. Now we come to the elderly folks. They have been around the block a time or two. They have attended the "school of fools" for many years and have finally learned (some of them have) that it isn't what you have or want in the outer that counts, but how you love and accept from within.

Then we observe the person who just seems to have "it." If you picture him in your mind's eye, you will see certain things about him. He doesn't condemn others; he doesn't judge others; he enjoys life and everyone in it — that is love. He is a walking, talking example of love in action.

And *you* can do exactly the same thing. You can change your life and your world. It is not too difficult to accomplish, provided you want to and you are willing to make the effort. You must activate creative responsibility into your life and world. Begin by consciously not condemning or judging any person or situation. Control your reactions! When someone does something, says something, or appears out of step to you, STOP! Remember that regardless of what he is doing or is not doing, he is handling his life and challenges in the best way he is able, according to his understanding. Whether you approve or disapprove of his actions is of little or no importance. It is *his* life and *his* problem. Don't make it your problem by jduging or condemning. For by condemning or judging him, you are only cluttering your own mind with his problem. And if you are like most of us, you have enough on your hands without taking on someone else's problems as well.

Even though it is sometimes an effort, consciously take time to "love him, bless him, and let him go."

Now that you are dealing properly with the other person, take time for you. Give yourself at least what you are willing to give the other fellow. Stop judging and condemning yourself for past actions and words. Love yourself, bless yourself, and let the past go. You are doing the best you know how to do according to your present understanding; just as in the past you did your best at that level of understanding. Love yourself and accept yourself right where you are. And don't worry—you won't be there long.

XI

Creating Health

THE NATURAL STATE of your body is health. Your body is wonderfully made and is wholly competent to heal and keep itself healthy. Your Creator did not create you and "plunk" you on earth with no provision for maintenance. This would be like General Motors manufacturing a fine automobile and not providing a method of servicing and maintaining it.

Contrary to popular belief, a medical doctor cannot heal you, nor can a "spiritual healer" make you well. This is not to say that they don't or can't play an important part in effecting a healing. Actually, the primary role of the physician is to create a physical environment that is conducive to healing. Healing is an inside job and the basic responsibility for a healing lies within the one being healed.

Your attitude toward health and healing has a great impact on your general health and how the healing process proceeds in your body. This is why one person has a rapid recovery from some condition, while another person with the same condition recovers more slowly. Those who recover rapidly usually have some basic attitudes in common:

1. They expect to get well quickly

2. They are relaxed and not up-tight about their condition

3. They are satisfied with the treatment they are receiving and with those who are administering the treatment

4. They have a reason to get well

All of these attitudes are chosen by the individual and anyone can adopt these attitudes if he so chooses.

The key to health lies in your response to and your opinion of your health and your body. A laceration on your back, where you cannot see it, will usually heal faster than the one that you can look at, form opinions about, and check on. In a sense, your body's innate intelligence or healing power can work unimpeded by your negative opinion of what is going on. Generally speaking, we all are about as healthy or unhealthy as we expect to be. This can be seen in the instance of the common cold. This is another one of those subjects that gets lots of attention verbally and in print. For some reason, people seem to enjoy talking about their annual cold pattern or forecast. For the most part, these people fall into three general categories:

1. "The All Winter Saga"
   This is the person who says, "As soon as the first frost (or snow or rain, depending on

where he lives) comes, I catch cold and I have it all winter long.'' Watch this person, and as soon as that first frost comes, his nose turns red and stays that way all winter.

2. ''The He-Man''
    This is the person who says, "I haven't had a cold in thirty years. I just never catch cold!" Enough said. He never catches cold.

3. "The Spring Whopper"
    This person says, "I almost never have a cold — except in the spring. And every spring I catch a whopper." Sure as spring, he has a "Spring Whopper."

You can be healthy and you can be healed. If you are under the care of a physician, follow his advice; he certainly knows more about the body and can creatively respond to the needs of your body and bring it to the level of health that you desire and expect. This can be most effectively accomplished by imaging the desired result.

Let's say, for example, that you are an avid tennis player and you suffer a fractured bone in your arm. Your physician treats you and then informs you that you may not be able to play tennis again because of the kind of fracture involved. Accept the fact that you have a fractured arm and follow the directions given you by the physician, but you do not have to accept the prognosis that you will not be able to play tennis.

Don't argue with the doctor and don't go around telling everyone what he said. Instead, add your own
inner treatment to his outer treatment. Spend a few
moments twice a day, seeing yourself playing tennis
with no limitations. Be specific in your imaging. See
yourself playing well, enjoying it and even winning.
Always think and image in terms of what you *want,*
not what you *do not want.*

There is no question that health and healings are
physical in nature, yet what we think and feel about
them is also vitally important. Our intellectual and
emotional states have profound effects on our health
in general and how we recover from illnesses and acci-
dents. The state of perfect health and the attaining of
good health is an inside job—physically, mentally,
and emotionally.

You are the product of what you think. Your words
are verbal expressions of what you think. Often
people say that they spoke without thinking, and yet,
this is not possible. They may not have consciously
considered what they have said, but thinking is an
integral part of speaking. It is important, then, to be
aware and careful about the words and phrases we
speak. There are phrases that become habits of speech
that should be avoided even if you don't really mean
them, or you are using them in a joking manner. Remember, your subconscious mind, that is always
striving to attain goals for you, does not make judgments or have a sense of humor. It accepts whatever
you give it as the gospel truth!

The kinds of phrases to avoid:
"She makes me sick."
"He gives me a pain in the neck."
"I'm too tired to move."
"I catch cold easily."
"Oh, my aching back."
"Heart trouble runs in my family."

Choose your words carefully today. Make sure they are pure and good, for tomorrow you may have to eat them.

All too often parents, without even being aware of what they are doing, transmit these kinds of thinking and speaking habits to their children under the guise of love. If a person seems to catch cold quite often, it is very likely that his mother may have said to him, "Put on a coat so you won't catch cold," or "Don't get wet, you'll catch pneumonia." She was looking out for his welfare out of love, but the goal-seeds that were planted were "cold" and "pneumonia." It would be far more constructive and just as effective to say, "Put on a coat so you'll be nice and warm," or "Stay dry and you'll be a lot more comfortable." In both instances, the parent is teaching a couple of lessons but in the first instance the teaching tool was fear (negative) and in the second, the tool was reward (positive). In the second instance the goal-seeds were "warm" and "comfortable," and these are worthy goals.

Most physicians agree that the vast majority of illnesses are psychosomatic. The basic cause of most illness is in the activity of the mind. One of the most obvious examples of this is stomach ulcers. They are usually the result of mental stress, worry, and anxiety. Other disorders that are caused by thinking may very well be more subtle and more difficult to pinpoint and identify with a particular thought habit. Look at it this way—a person can be generally negative in his outlook on life; generally anxious much of the time; worry about everything in general, but the body does not become ill or break down *generally*. The body must react *specifically*. It is not just an idea or a thought or a feeling; the human body is a tangible entity that can only demonstrate specifically— specific symptoms, good or bad.

Your health is the product of your thinking. If you want better health and more vitality, you must change the way you think about your body. The choice is yours. And you are not alone in this return to health. Health is your natural state and the word *heal* means, "To restore to original purity or integrity." There is a power in you to heal you, that is beyond the scope of your total understanding. Yet, it is there and it is at work constantly. Albert Einstein said, "Everyone who is seriously involved in the pursuit of science becomes convinced that a spirit is manifest in the laws of the universe—a spirit vastly superior to that of man, and one in the face of which we, with our modest powers, must feel humble."

The power is there within you and you can work with it through the positive activity of your mind.

XII

Prosperity

TO MANY PEOPLE, the accumulation of wealth, having money, and the things money can buy or just being prosperous, is some kind of sin. Religion has done its share to convince people that it is somehow honorable and spiritual to be poor. Yet, there is far more in the Bible to assure man of his right to prosperity than a right or distinction to be impoverished. If there is a "sin" involved here, the "sin" is in poverty—not prosperity. Our Bible has over eighty-five references to riches, and a closer look reveals that virtually all of the great characters of the Old Testament were materially rich. It is spiritually all right for you to prosper! Poverty or lack of any kind need not be a part of you or your life.

You can change your level of prosperity by changing your mind. You can make up your mind to prosper and there is only one limit to the amount of prosperity you can attain. That one limit is placed by you on yourself. The limit is also affected by how you choose to think and talk about your financial affairs. Your prosperity comes from within you, not from outside of you!

Much like a physical healing, your prosperity is an "inside job," and is affected very little by outside events. What you *think* about outside events *does* affect your prosperity. In order to have prosperity in your life, you must begin to create it within before it can be manifested and made spendable.

All too often we get into unproductive thinking habits that literally keep our prosperity away from us. People say, "I think about money all day, but I don't seem to be getting any richer." Yet, in reality, if they would examine their thoughts, they would discover that they are thinking about the *lack* of money. If you keep thinking of a lack of money, that is precisely what you get — more lack of money.

I CAN'T AFFORD

These three little words, "I can't afford," cause far more inability to afford than the financial situations they supposedly describe. More often than not, they are a "little white lie" used as a cop-out, rather than stating a fact. If someone asks you to join them for dinner and a movie, and you simply would rather not go with them, an easy out is to say, "I can't afford it this week." Yet, the fact is that you could afford it if you really wanted to go. Okay, you have been polite and not hurt anybody's feelings, but you have planted another solid "I can't afford" seed (goal) in your subconscious mind. Think how much more productive for you and how much more honest to have said, "Thank you for asking, but I'd rather not. I have some things I want to get done."

So often "I can't afford," in either speech or thought, is used when other phrases would be creatively more constructive as well as more accurate. Better statements would be:

"I don't choose to spend my money for that."

"I have a priority list and that is not a high priority in my life now."

"No thank you."

"I don't care to buy that."

Usually, even when we know we can afford something, we tend to say, "I can't afford" to a salesperson (especially an aggressive one). It may seem like an easy out, but it is a costly one in terms of goal setting. You really can't afford to say, "I can't afford."

A RAINY DAY

Our non-productive thinking habits, especially about money, are habits we have formed out of our responses to people around us and their opinions of the source of prosperity. Often our parents are our greatest teachers in this area, especially if they came from a below average income family, or if they experienced the depression of the late 1920's and early 1930's. The habits approach and take hold very subtly but very securely. One thinking-habit that has been handed down through generations in many families is the stated reason for saving money, "I'm saving for a rainy day."

Save money for a "rainy day," and you set a goal for a "rainy day." The variations of the "rainy day" thinking-habit are many. "I'm saving money in case I get sick and can't work." "I'm saving money in case I get laid off from my job." "When we go on strike I'll need the money."

Why not save money for something you *want?* Saving money is all well and good, but save it for a constructive goal: a vacation, a new home, a new car, or a trip around the world. Just be sure you are saving for something you *want.*

Your prosperity must first be established in your mind. This is perfectly logical, for if you look around you, you will not see anything that did not begin as an idea in mind. It follows then that your prosperity must be established in *your* mind first.

It is vitally important that *you* accept the responsibility for your prosperity or your lack of prosperity. As long as you give that responsibility or any part of it to someone or something other than you, your own creativity is stifled. If you blame the government, your employer, your parents, the economy, your childhood, or the stars, you have relinquished your own creative responsibility. And *your* creative responsibility should be one of your most treasured possessions. It is yours—don't give it away.

We have been told that the Bible states "money is the root of all evil," yet, this is not exactly true. It is not even the complete sentence being quoted. The complete statement is, "The *love* of money is the root of all evil." Money in itself has no power. It is a thing with little or no intrinsic value and can do nothing without our help. The power attributed to money is the result of what people *think* and *believe* about money. What people *think* and *believe* is a choice each one makes for himself. It is also said that often people love money and use people, instead of using money and loving people. There is no doubt that this is true, but once again it is an individual choice. We choose what we will think about money or anything else and what we think about is what we bring forth into our world.

You have just as much right to prosperity as any other person on this planet, but it is *your* responsibility to bring it into your life. It is an inside job that begins with you and within you. Open your mind to prosperity and put your creative process to work for *your* good.

XIII

Creating Prosperity

THERE ARE MANY techniques to help you change how you think about money and prosperity in general. As you change your mind, your prosperity level changes too. Reading about these techniques or even memorizing them will do nothing to change your status. You must make the decision to "work" these techniques in order to change you. The buck stops here! No one can do it for you. Use the techniques, don't judge them, rationalize them, or cast them aside because they seem so simple. Remember! The goal is to change your thought-habits that are well entrenched in your subconscious mind. You may think your thought-habits do not need changing, but this is only true if you have all the material good you want. (If this *is* true for you, skip this chapter, you don't need it.) All of the techniques discussed in this chapter are designed to reinforce your creative responses to the point where you begin to respond automatically and positively. This is little more than training your mind through discipline to respond creatively and increase your prosperity level.

WANT LIST

Become definite about what you want or desire. Put it down in writing. Make a list of the things you would most like to have. Rearrange the list so that it becomes a list of priorities. Make the thing you want most number one on the list and let the other items follow in order of importance to you. Don't list things according to the price. Let some of the items be immediate needs or wants and some be longer-range goals. A sample list for a woman might be:

1. Matching bath mat and towels
2. Vacuum cleaner
3. Full length fur coat
4. New living room set
5. Bicycle
6. Swimming lessons
7. AM-FM digital clock radio

The list may be considerably longer, but should not be shorter.

Read the list over at least twice a day, adding or deleting as your desires dictate. Cross out anything you get. Rearrange your priorities if you wish and rewrite your list from time to time.

Right along with this "want list" begin a "thank you list." Each time you receive something from the "want list" or something that wasn't itemized on the list, write it on the "thank you list." Work with both lists on an on-going basis. Let your lists be items that are always in your wallet or purse.

Do not share the list with others. It is *not* a "hint" list. You are working on your consciousness of prosperity, not advertising what you want. Remember, prosperity is an "inside job."

PAY YOUR BILLS

If you ever find yourself worrying about paying bills or perhaps one particular bill that has been of great concern to you — "pay your bills." In the realm of your imagination — "pay your bills." After you are in bed and the lights are out, take out all your bills, your check book and start writing the checks in your imagination! In your mind's eye "see" the checks and "see" yourself writing them in detail. Write across each bill, "Paid in full." Put each bill and check in the proper envelope, address it, put a stamp on it, seal it, and mail it off. In your imagination go through the entire process confidently, joyously, just as though you had all the money needed to pay all those bills.

Not only is this an effective goal-establishing method, but it is also just as effective as counting sheep, and far more creative.

PICTURES

Get a picture of what you want and put it up where you see it every day. Make certain it is a picture of what you want specifically. If you want a particular automobile, get a picture of the make, model, and year. If it is a house, find a picture that comes as close as possible to what you want. If it is a camera, be specific. Put the picture (or pictures) where *you* are sure to see it daily — on the refrigerator door, under the glass on your desk, in the top of your briefcase, or on your bathroom mirror. A dollar value for weekly, monthly, or annual salary is a valid "picture," but a picture of an object has greater impact.

This concept of putting up a picture of what you want is certainly not a new one. It goes back before history. Early man drew pictures of successful hunts on the walls of caves that he called home. The Egyptians, of thousands of years past, carved and drew scenes of wealth and happiness, successful hunts, bountiful crops and victories in battle on the walls of the tombs that were begun when a child was born. North American Indians recorded things of the past and things yet to come in sand paintings and the decoration of teepees. It is an age-old technique that still works.

When you see the picture and you have a moment, mentally possess it, use it, and admire it. But do *not* think about *how* you got it or how you might be able to get it. That is the work of your subconscious goal-achieving activity. Your job is to hold the mental image.

Give Thanks

Giving thanks is one of the most effective ways of increasing the flow of good into your life. Virtually every religious philosophy in the world places great emphasis on giving thanks, and it works. It is effective for two very practical reasons. First, it establishes a positive attitude of mind because it makes you more aware of what you *have* instead of what you don't have. Secondly, it reinforces or proves that you can create and have created prosperity—everything you now have, began within you!

If you think that the past year has not been particularly good for you, sit down with paper and pencil and make a list of *everything* you have acquired during the year and give thanks for it as you write it down. Don't be surprised if the year turns out to be far better than you had judged it.

Another good exercise is one that should be done at least once a month. Begin by standing in the middle of your living room, look at everything in the room and give thanks for it. Don't miss anything: the rug you are standing on, the lamps, the ashtray, and every picture on the wall. Be thorough and give thanks for everything! When you have completed the living-room, move to another room and do exactly the same thing. Give thanks for everything. Go through every room in this manner and you will find how much you really do have to be thankful for. In everything give thanks!

Prosperity is truly an attitude of mind, and because it is, how much you have materially is governed by your attitude about prosperity and your attitude about your right and ability to be prosperous. Create the things you *want* in your life. Don't allow yourself to become bogged down with the prophets of doom, because here we are—each succeeding generation is bigger, healthier, happier, living longer and more affluently. This is a good world, a good life, and things just keep getting better because man is innately creative in his responses to his life and his world.

XIV

Happiness Never "Happens"

HAPPINESS IS ONE of the most sought after goals of mankind and yet the ingredients of happiness are as varied as the individuals who seek it.

Happiness might be living in a marble palace, lounging around on a pile of cushions and being waited on hand and foot.

Or it might be having two chauffeured limousines, a closet full of furs, the biggest house in town and money to burn.

Or perhaps it is being free from sickness, problems, and frustrations.

Or maybe you're easy to please, like Charlie Brown, and happiness is a warm puppy.

Happiness is a very personal and subjective thing. No one has come up with a cut-and-dried blueprint of what makes up happiness. No one ever will because happiness is the result of response-patterns or habits within the individual. Like most habits, your response-habits are from the subconscious. Happiness is the result of a good or creative response-habit, just as unhappiness is the result of poor or non-creative response-habits. Fortunately response-habits can be changed.

Happiness (or unhappiness) never just "happens," it is created step by step, thought by thought, according to each person's opinions and responses to the world and everything in it. Abraham Lincoln said, "Most people are as happy as they make up their minds to be."

How happy do you want to be?

Being happy is *not* being without problems.

Happiness does not mean—not having a care in the world.

Happiness is knowing *how* to solve problems!

Happiness is *not* sitting around not doing anything, but rather knowing how to put the joy of living into everything you do—including the drudgery. You can be happy or happier if *you* make up your mind to be.

Your happiness or your unhappiness is your responsibility and only you can change your state of happiness.

UNHAPPINESS IS LEARNED

Happiness is your natural and normal state and you can be happy if you allow yourself to be. We *learn* to be unhappy as children and get better and better at it as we grow up. In a very true sense we become successfully miserable. We learn to be unhappy, or find out what makes us unhappy, from our parents, our peers, and from what we glean from news media, television and motion pictures. As children and teenagers, we tended to choose as yardsticks for our happiness, the same yardsticks used by those closest to us. As very young children, we learned very well, with little or no independent thought or rational questioning. We established definite, but not necessarily valid, rules for what will make us happy or unhappy. Too often these accepted rules or guidelines for happiness are not challenged by the adult mind and reevaluated. Instead, the adult continues to be unhappy —blaming others, conditions, and governments for his circumstances—and never makes an effort to change what he thinks.

Some of the guidelines for happiness are learned very young and very well by children, just as prejudices are learned quite young. We adults wonder at, and yet readily accept, how a child who is placed in a foreign language environment quickly and easily picks up the language with no formal training. With an open and curious mind, he quickly adapts to a new speech habit which is automatically a thinking habit. Consider for a moment how many other thinking habits each child quickly and easily adopts in his own environment. Certainly many of those thinking habits are useful, but many are invalid and literally destructive to the child's future happiness.

If you find that there is too much unhappiness in your life, then it is time to check your responses and to what you are responding.

HAPPINESS IS NOW

A vast number of people place their happiness in some future time, place, condition, or event. They literally put off their happiness, not realizing that they can have it NOW. They seem to be always on the very brink of happiness with one hurdle to overcome:

> "I'll be happy when we have our own home."
>
> "I'll be happy when we get out of this house and into a condominium with no yard-work and maintenance to do."
>
> "Everything will be wonderful when I get married and have my own family."
>
> "I'll be happy once I get through this divorce and have my freedom."

This list goes on and on: new job, new town, out of town, get all the children in school, get all the children out of school, or whatever is a convenient time or event off in the future.

Your happiness is *not* dependent on any event in the future. Your happiness is dependent solely on your response to your world today. Change your opinion and your response *today* and you change your level of happiness today.

No One Can Make You Happy

So often we hear people say or infer that they are foregoing their own happiness for the present time in order that another person will be happy. Others believe that to seek one's own happiness before another's is selfish. Then there are those who say, "She makes me happy," or "He makes me unhappy." None of these statements is true! In a very real sense they are excuses that are rather poor excuses at best.

Remember the next two statements, they are vital to *your* happiness:

> *You can't make another person happy or unhappy.*

> *Another person cannot make you happy or unhappy.*

For all practical purposes there are no exceptions to those statements. Accept them at face value without trying to bend them around to fit specific situations. You cannot make another person happy or unhappy, simply because happiness is the result of the individual's mental attitude which he alone controls. And exactly the same is true of your happiness. You control your attitudes and your responses.

It is not selfish to seek happiness for yourself first. As a matter of fact, it is important for you to seek your happiness first. If someone asks you for a sum of money, the very first question that must be answered within you is, "Do I have that sum of money?" Unless that question is answered in the affirmative, any and all other questions are academic. You cannot give something you do not have. Exactly the same is true of anything else you would share with another human being; love, respect, trust, understanding, or happiness. You cannot share these priceless gifts with another until *you* have them.

Happiness is a habit—a very good habit. Happiness is a mental attitude—a very good mental attitude. In the event that you want more happiness in your life, don't try to rebuild and change things around in your physical world. Go to work on your attitudes and responses. You probably know of a situation or individual that seems to bring forth an unhappy response from you. Take a moment right now to bring that person or situation to mind. *Don't* ask yourself why this person makes you unhappy. Rather, ask yourself, "Why do I *choose* to respond with unhappiness in this instance?" or, "Why do I *believe* I must be unhappy under these circumstances?"

Epictetus said, "Men are disturbed not by things that happen, but by their opinion of the things that happen." The choice is yours, and happiness can be yours beginning this moment. Your happiness can and will be a great gift to those around you. Happiness is a habit and it is a contagious habit.

XV

Relax — Be Cool

IT CAN BE quite fascinating to look into words; how they change in meaning, what their counter-part is in other languages, and how we use them. Simple words can have totally diverse meanings to people within one culture.

In a class-room situation of adult, middle-class, urban people, I tested the idea that simple words mean different things to different people. They were asked to write down the first definition or synonym that came to mind. The word was "cat." Most people had a definition relating to a feline of some kind. However, four men wrote, "bulldozer," two women answered, "gossip," and one man, who was reading an historical novel about sailing ships, answered "whip" (cat-of-nine-tails).

Words change through usage and words change as a result of translations. The Bible is no exception and often through translations, words get changed. Many people of the Christian faith have been bothered by the statement of Jesus that says, "Blessed are the meek for they shall inherit the earth." In our culture "meekness" implies weakness, passivity, a kind of "Mr. Milktoast" quality. Certainly it is not a trait one would seek to cultivate. Now, in the French language Bible, the word is translated as "debonair." According to the dictionary, "debonair" is defined with words like courteous, with pleasant manners, carefree and charming. In common usage we think of a man as being debonair if he is well-mannered, at ease in most all situations, poised and, in the vernacular, "cool." With this in mind, a possible translation might very well be, "Blessed are the cool for they shall inherit the earth."

Stop and think! The people that you know, or know of, who are successful in their lives are "cool." They are "at ease" in almost any situation. Then look at yourself. You are always at your very best when you are at ease. You are always able to speak better, think more clearly, and act more decisively when there is no pressure, no one threatening you, and you are at ease. Relax, take it easy, keep cool, and you will have the kind of life you desire.

Set your goal. See that goal complete in your mind's eye, and hold to it. Do the best you can in the outer and then relax. Let it happen. Allow your mind the freedom to create what you want in life.

Don't try to make yourself relax. *Let* yourself relax. Start with the muscles of your body and let them relax. Begin with your toes and work up to your facial muscles and tongue. Let them relax. When your body is relaxed, when the muscles are kept at rest, you cannot be angry, afraid, or anxious.

When you analyze what makes you fearful, angry,

or up-tight, you find it is not the event, circumstance, or person that causes the emotion. The emotion is caused by your response or opinion of the event, circumstance, or person. No one or no thing can make you tense; it is your choice of responses. By the same token, no one or no thing can make you relax. Again, it is your choice.

Practice relaxing your body consciously on a regular basis. Let it rest easy as you creatively use your imagination.

Your "Secret Place"

You, like every other person in the world, need a "place" where you can be alone. A place where no other person can ever intrude. Many, many people have such a "place"; the concept is widely taught, and has been taught down through the ages.

This "place"—this "secret place"—is in the realm of your mind, created especially for you by you. It is a place to which you can retreat whenever you choose. It should be created carefully and specifically for your comfort and ease. It can be a room, a garden, an ocean shore, or as Jesus called it—a closet.

If, for you, it is a room, then create the room in detail in whatever way is meaningful to you. Remember, no one else can ever enter your "secret place." Make sure that it is pleasing to you and comfortable. Take time to go regularly to your "secret place" and get away from the world around you. Relax and be at peace with yourself.

I have a friend who has a large trash-can just

outside his "secret place" in which he deposits all his problems and hassles *before* he enters. He says, "I don't want all of that garbage in my room. I go there to get *away* from it." That's sound advice! Don't litter your "secret place." It is a place in which to relax, be at peace, and to contemplate the creative genius that dwells within you.

My "secret place" has been the same place for many years, and I created it in a time of personal need. It is not a room but a short stretch of beach in Southern California. There is a line of short pilings marching straight into the surf, remnants of a long-forgotten pier. Just above the high tide line there is a bank of sand, a perfect back rest for a solitary dreamer. I've been there so often, I can hear the gulls, watch the busy snipe, smell the salt, and occasionally watch a fishing boat just beyond the breakers.

Escapism? Perhaps, but so is fine music, trite television, and so is sleep. We all need to escape from time to time. We need to let our bodies rest and relax and we need to let our minds do the same. Your mind cannot effectively create when it is fatigued any more than your muscles can work effectively when they are fatigued.

As you read these last few words, remember, the mind that is perceiving, judging, and filing away these words, is the most complex, creative, and most powwerful force in the universe.

Use it! It is yours! Respond creatively and have the good that is rightfully yours!